ETIQUETTE

for the *Career Woman*

ETIQUETTE

for the *Career Woman*

All the **Wisdom, Wit** and **Advice**
you will ever need to attain
Personal *and* **Professional Excellence**

Jolienne Moore and **Lynn Cris**

Cover Art: Brent Hallwachs and Darrick Monin
Interior Art: Darrick Monin

• **Modella Books** •
A division of Modella Enterprises Inc.

Modella Books
A division of Modella Enterprises Inc.

For information about special discounts for bulk purchases or on consulting services for your business, school, or organization please contact: Modella Enterprises Inc. at info@modellabooks.com

Cover Art: Brent Hallwachs and Darrick Monin
Interior Art: Darrick Monin

Printed in USA & Canada

Library and Archives Canada Cataloguing in Publication

Moore, Jolienne
    Etiquette for the career woman : all the wisdom, wit and advice you will ever need to attain personal and professional excellence / Jolienne Moore and Lynn Cris.

Includes bibliographical references.
ISBN 978-0-9867499-0-2

1. Etiquette for women. I. Cris, Lynn II. Title.

BJ1876.M66 2010   395.1'44   C2010-906642-1

For my husband Richard, our son Parker
and the rest of my supportive family,
with love and gratitude

"Excellence has a shadow, it's called Success."

Jolienne Moore

For Tudor, Alexandriana and Bianca;
thank you for your support and love
always.

"Belief and Will are more important then skill."

Lynn Cris

CONTENTS

THE TEN PRINCIPLES OF
Excellence

Your Foundation For Life

1. I am 100% responsible for my communication.

2. Everyone is doing the best he or she can.

3. I respect each person's model of the world.

4. There is no failure, only feedback.

5. Flexibility brings power.

6. Everything in my world is a reflection of me.

7. My thoughts create my reality.

8. Energy flows where attention goes.

9. All power comes from within.

10. Live in the present.

Used with permission: Lynn Robinson,
The Robinson Group

INTRODUCTION

When it comes to etiquette there is more to it than a strict set of rules that you must memorize and practice to perfection. The premise behind all rules of etiquette is making others feel good and living your best life by living with excellence.

If you find yourself in a situation where you are unsure of the rules of etiquette remember this... when in doubt consider those around you. Do what will make them most comfortable and put them at ease.

Being successful is easy; the more value you create for others, the more personal success will come your way.

Conversational Etiquette

"Good communication is as stimulating as black coffee, and just as hard to sleep after."

Anne Morrow Lindbergh

"The real art of conversation is not only to say the right thing at the right place but to leave unsaid the wrong thing at the tempting moment."

Dorothy Nevill

Our words are extremely powerful. The words we use have the ability to lift people up, alter moods and inspire excellence. They can determine how we feel based on the emotional response we get when we hear them. Saying something is a 'total failure' versus 'an opportunity for improvement' gives a completely different feel.

Words contain vibration, an element of energy. That energy is present whether the words are written or spoken, in conversation or in our head. Our bodies respond to those vibrations physically at a cellular level by way of resonance (the act of vibration resulting in more vibration) so much so, that the kind of life we have is determined by how we use words, and how we relate to the meanings we assign them based on our beliefs and filters.

Those beliefs and filters begin developing from birth. Everything we are ever told, every experience we have, helps to shape those beliefs. We begin to see the world not as it actually is but as we believe it to be based on how it appears to us.

1

When we are exposed to positive words and thoughts, our bodies respond with health and well-being. Negative words adversely affect our bodies and our energetic vibration resulting in disease and lack.

Internationally renowned researcher and author Dr. Masaru Emoto has published several great books with photographic evidence on the effect words have on water and our bodies (which consist of about 70% water). He shows how exposing water to words of high positive vibration such as "Love" and "Gratitude" and then freezing it causes the water to form beautiful balanced crystals. Exposing the exact same water to negative words such as "Stupid" or "That's no good" causes the crystals to turn out broken and deformed.

Purifying the water in our bodies and improving our health and well being is easy; simply making a habit of using positive words on a daily basis is a great start! Use expressions such as "Thank you" often, and focus on things that you love rather than noticing what you don't like about people, places and events. Use your words to encourage and inspire instead of to gossip and complain.

Limit your exposure to negative vibrations on the radio, TV and in conversation. Keep in mind that even negative words used in humour are still negative in vibration. Choose to shift your attention and seek out the positive. Before long you will find that you have tipped the scale and are attracting more positive experiences into your life.

I choose not to watch the news or read the newspapers, as for the most part they focus on negative events that leave me feeling less than wonderful. Instead I read books and watch programs that leave me feeling great and inspired and therefore that becomes my reality.

RESPECT

"There was no respect for youth when I was young, and now that I am old, there is no respect for age –I missed it coming and going."

John B. Priestly

▶ It should go without saying but until we get to the point where it actually does, treat everyone you come in contact with with full respect regardless of who they are. Respect others' models of the world and remember that everyone is doing the best he or she can in the moment.

▶ Pay attention to your choice of words and choose not to participate in gossip.

▶ Chose to live with integrity. When you say you will do something be sure to follow through.

▶ Be sincere. If you say, "We should get together for coffee," show you mean it and follow up with the person within two to three days.

▶ When paying your respects to a person who has lost someone close to them, keep it short and sincere. Tell them how sorry you are to hear of the sad news and how much the deceased will be missed. A card to let them know you are there for them is a thoughtful gesture.

"Men are respectable only as they respect."

Ralph Waldo Emerson

INTRODUCTIONS

"Do you suppose I could buy back my introduction to you?"

Groucho Marx

A great host is one who can fill a room with strangers and within minutes have everyone chatting like they were old friends.

She is a connector, drawing attention to the link between degrees of separation. She has a keen ability for bringing people together and making strategic alliances.

What is her secret?

She has mastered the art of introductions; a skill that carries over to every facet of life from social gatherings to networking events and is a valuable tool for every career woman.

A professional introduction puts everyone at ease and paves the way for conversation. It creates rapport and a strong foundation from which future business transactions and friendships may transpire.

When it comes to introductions there are some basic rules that are easy to follow. The most important of which is to actually do it! Once you remember to take that first important step, there are a few more points to consider in order to ensure it will be an effective introduction.

▶ Mention the name of the person you most wish to impress first.

For example:
You are walking down the street with a colleague Lynn, and you meet a very good client of yours, Donna Smith...

"Donna, I'd like you to meet my colleague, Lynn Cris. Lynn, this is Donna Smith."

In this case continuing to make a good impression on Donna Smith is important as she is the client.

▶ Normally you would introduce a younger person to an older one and a coworker to a client (as in the example above).

Inserting the word 'to' into the introduction means you would then reverse the order of the names in order to stay consistent with the rule.

"Miss Young, I'd like to introduce you <u>to</u> Mrs. Older"
OR
"Mrs. Older, I'd like you to meet Miss Young,"

When introducing someone else, be sure to use their credentials such as "Dr." When introducing yourself, leave those credentials off.

▶ During an introduction, add a tidbit of information such as where the person works. This gives everyone a starting point from which a conversation can follow.

"Donna, I'd like you to meet my friend, Lynn Cris from Modella Me. Lynn, this is Donna Smith, Principal of Grove Middle School'."

▶ They will think of you all the more fondly if you take it a step further and get the conversation going in a direction that is of potential interest to both of them.

"This is great. I was just telling Donna the other day about you and the amazing work you do to help build confidence in kids. Donna is a huge advocate for anti-bullying and is always looking to find new ways to instill confidence in her students. I was thinking I should arrange to connect the two of you and now here we are! I always say there is no such thing as a coincidence."

Once you have set up the conversation you can exit knowing that the introduction is complete and your acquaintances are on their way to exercising their conversation skills.

▶ When you are at a business gathering and would like to introduce your spouse (Richard) to the company President (Mrs. Sidney Green) it would go something like this...

"Mrs. Green, I would like you to meet my husband, Richard. Richard, meet Sidney Green, President of Green Interiors."

FORGOTTEN NAME

▶ If you have forgotten someone's name, simply ask them politely to remind you.

   "My memory is not serving me well today, I'm sorry; I've forgotten your name."

▶ If someone forgets your name while introducing you, smile, extend your hand and introduce yourself. Be sure to set the other person at ease by making light of the situation.

▶ If the person making the introduction mispronounces your name or gives out any incorrect information, make the correction promptly and politely.

▶ To remember the name of someone you are being introduced to, repeat the name while you are shaking hands. Be sure to use the name again during conversation to solidify it in your memory. If you are a visual person picture the name in written form in your mind. If it's a unique name you may find it helpful to ask how it's spelled by saying something like "What a pretty name, does it have a unique spelling?"

HANDSHAKE

"You cannot shake hands with a clenched fist."

Indira Gandhi

A handshake may seem obvious; however, with the number of poor handshakes we have experienced and the important role a handshake plays on first impressions it is definitely worth covering!

One of my clients was a man from Korea who hired me to help him learn North American customs and Business Etiquette.

The first thing I noticed upon meeting him was his delicate handshake. In his country a gentle handshake is standard, yet in North America he is expected to have a firm handshake as a weak one signals a lack of confidence. Knowing these differences can really help make a great first impression.

▶ A handshake should be firm, no limp fish please! This does not mean so firm that you crush the other persons hand though as this can signal a domineering personality.

▶ A medium-firm grip is acceptable. Be sure it is palm to palm and thumbs should interlock. A couple pumps with the arm are all that is needed.

▶ These days, in business it is acceptable to shake hands with both males and females; in fact it is expected.

▶ What if someone refuses your hand?

Simply withdraw your hand and continue your greeting. You have shown proper etiquette by extending your hand and you will continue to do so by maintaining your composure.

INTRODUCING YOURSELF

You aren't the only one feeling a little nervous at the social or networking events!

▶ Always stand when greeting someone.

▶ Set others at ease by taking the initiative to introduce yourself. Take a step forward with your arm extended toward them and your hand positioned ready to shake theirs as you look them in the eye and smile.

"A smile is a curve that sets everything straight."

Phyllis Diller

▶ Always introduce yourself using your **first** and **last** name. It's acceptable to ask the other person for their last name if they do not give it out. You can also use this as an opportunity to repeat their name a few times to help retain it in your memory.
"Sarah?" (Confirming you heard correctly)
"It's great to meet you!
What's your last name Sarah?"

"Confidence contributes more to conversation than wit."

François de la Rochefoucauld

SIMPLE STEPS TO ENCOURAGE CONVERSATION

1. **Smile** - Shows friendliness

2. **Open posture** - Avoid crossing your arms in front of you to appear more approachable.

3. **Eye contact** - Exhibits confidence

4. **Handshake** - Create a connection

5. **Lean in** - Leaning slightly forward shows interest in what the other person is saying.

6. **Nod** - Allows the other person to see that you are listening to what is being said.

ESTABLISHING RAPPORT

Being an expert at establishing rapport is a useful skill for anyone to perfect. Rapport is a process of connection and responsiveness. When people are alike they like each other and they feel at ease. The process of developing rapport enables us to achieve a sense of "likeness" by matching and mirroring through our physiology, tonality and the words we use.

Physiology plays the largest part in establishing rapport – 55% in fact. Matching and mirroring our body language, gestures, posture, expressions and even our breathing rate to one another, is an important step in creating a sense of ease.

Tonality (the speed, tone, volume and pace at which we speak) is the second most important element with 38% of it determining whether or not we successfully establish rapport. Interestingly enough, the experiences we have in common and the actual words and expressions we use only account for 7% of the ability to establish rapport. This is extremely exciting as it means we can still make an effective connection even with those we have nothing in common with. More connections mean more happy clients!

Potential clients seeking a particular product or service will often shop around. The competition may have similar merchandise but if you have the ability to connect with people you will have the upper hand. We all want to feel good about our buying decisions and much of that comes from feeling heard and understood by those we buy from. Really listening to what your clients are saying and following the rapport building techniques on the following page will ensure you both come away happy and successful.

Establishing Rapport for a Successful Outcome

1. **Know Your Intention** for the conversation and set your outcome (what you would like to achieve from the conversation).

2. **Take Action** – interact, greet, and begin conversation.

3. **Observe and Match** – Pay attention to the subtleties of the person's physiology, tonality, and words, and match and mirror yours to them. Subtlety is the key; don't make the other person uncomfortable by copying every movement.

4. **Ask Questions** - Take note of the feedback you are receiving. Ask questions to verify if the other party agrees with you. If they do, then you have successfully established rapport.

5. **Once Rapport is Established** you can begin leading the person in the direction of your outcome. Continue repeating the process to ensure they stay in agreement until you reach your successful outcome.

6. **Cycle Back to Agreement** if you are off track and not in rapport. If at any time you ask a question and do not receive agreement, rapport has been broken. At that point, with the outcome you originally set in mind, take your client back to the point where you last had agreement, regain rapport and carry on with the process until you reach your successful outcome.

"Don't knock the weather; nine-tenths of the people couldn't start a conversation if it didn't change once in a while."

Kin Hubbard

BUSINESS CARDS

▶ Always carry business cards with you. You never know when you will need one.

▶ Your business card is a representation of you.

▶ Keep your cards in good condition and avoid handing out ripped, wrinkled & stained cards.

▶ If you change your phone number or any information on your card, do not cross anything out and do not write your new information on the card. Get new cards!

▶ Only give out one card to someone unless they ask for more. You don't want to assume they will hand out your card for you.

▶ When you are given a business card, treat it like it is an extension of the person who has given it to you. Look at the card and acknowledge something about it that you like (the font, logo, colour). Be sure the compliment is genuine. Make people feel important, and in turn it will make you important to them.

▶ Never place a business card you have just been given in your back pocket. This is a sign of disrespect. Place it in your purse, card holder or jacket pocket.

▶ Business cards are normally given out at the beginning of a meeting. Keep the card out over the duration of the meeting to help you remember names.

For more information on business cards and International interactions see INTERNATIONAL ETIQUETTE.

Social Etiquette

"The elevator to success is out of order. You'll have to use the stairs... one step at a time."

Joe Girard

How we chose to conduct ourselves on a daily basis, whether on the job or in a social situation, determines a lot about our character, who we are, and what type of experiences and people we will attract into our lives. Our behaviour matches how we feel about ourselves.

To change our behaviour we must first change the way we think, as all thoughts result in an auto- response physiological representation. In other words, our thoughts and beliefs show up in our body language and actions.

93% of communication is non-verbal – That's right! Those little voices and the thoughts in your head that you think no one can hear are coming across louder than you think! … *"Uh Oh" is right!* What kind of message are you sending if you are judging someone or you are being critical of yourself?

CHANGE YOUR THOUGHTS TO CHANGE YOUR RESULTS!
It's as simple as that.

The first thoughts we have as we wake up and the last thoughts before bed have a large impact on what will take place throughout the hours in between. Thinking about how busy and stressful your day is going to be will only cause you to attract more things that make it even busier and more stressful. Instead, if you have a full day ahead and need energy, pop in your favorite disco song and groove it out - Travolta style! Do anything that makes you feel good. After all, we do create our reality through our feelings, thoughts and words.

When we feel good we send out positive energy vibrations that in turn attract more things, people, and circumstances with the same positive vibration.

We are magnets attracting to us that which we give out. The Law of Attraction is a scientifically proven Law of the Universe. Simply put, the Law of Attraction states that like attracts like, so if we see and think about that which we love we will receive more of what we love. If we focus on what we don't want, guess what? We get more of what we don't want! We can only attract things, people and events that are on the same vibration as we are.

Does that make you think twice before complaining about poor customer service and the person who cut you off in traffic?

There are reasons why some people have such great lives and others seem to have constant struggle. "Stuff" doesn't just happen; everything we receive in our lives is based on what we've given.

If you have negative thoughts and feelings about your job then you will attract difficult clients and negative experiences that cause you to dislike your job even more. If you look for the positive things about your job then you will draw more positive experiences and satisfied clients to you giving cause to love it even more.

Start your day off on the right track the moment you wake up. Waking up to a favorite song or a morning meditation CD really helps to balance your energy and put you in the right frame of mind for the rest of your day. Much more relaxing than waking with a jump to beeping alarms or ringing bells! Hello stress!

▶ Get a CD alarm clock and set it for an hour earlier than you normally get up.

(Did we just hear a "yeah right" from those of you who think of yourselves as non-morning people? You know who you are!)

Start by changing your self-talk to tell yourself that you ARE a morning person and look for things you can love about getting up early. *(Before you bypass this section of the book, just give it a week; speaking as a former non-morning person, you'll be amazed!)*

Getting up an hour earlier everyday over the course of a month is an extra thirty free hours! Use it to do something that brings you joy and makes you feel good. *(Thirty waking hours is more than many people get in a weekend! Just imagine what you can do with an extra weekend every month!)*

Don't let another morning of getting up on the wrong side of the bed wreak havoc on your day. Get your day off to a good start by making sure you are feeling and thinking positively before you even get out of bed. That way there won't be a 'wrong side of the bed' to get up on!

▶ While you are still in bed think of at least ten things that you love and are grateful for: before you know it mornings will seem a whole lot better. As you continue looking for things you love and are thankful for throughout the day you'll find that you will start to attract even more of what you love.

▶ Look for things you can love even in things that normally would irritate you. If you focus on what you love you can't even see what you don't like as you aren't on the same vibration as it is.

RESONANCE

Our resonance, the level of vibration we produce in response to external stimuli, is the result of our vibration connecting with the like vibration of others. This resonance is extremely powerful as it directly affects the level of success we will achieve in all areas of our lives.

Just as one vibrating tuning fork will cause another nearby tuning fork of the same frequency to make the same sound, we will respond to the vibrations of the people we are the closest to, causing us to resonate on the same frequency and produce similar or like results.

What does this mean? The people we spend the majority of our time and energy with (namely the top five people) have a huge influence over our resonance (how high or low our vibrations will be) and in turn, the results we see in our lives, (our success or lack there of).

On average our level of success falls within 20% of the level achieved by those closest to us as we naturally elevate or drop to the level of our peers. This goes for every area of our lives including health, relationships, spirituality, personal development, sense of humor, career, and even income, all will be within 20% of those top five people!

▶ Limit the amount of time you spend in the presence of those who keep you stuck by projecting their doubts and fears (low vibrations) onto you with statements such as "That will never work". Instead, choose to surround yourself with successful people who encourage and support your growth.

▶ Spend time with people who excel in specific areas, doing activities that represent the areas they are strongest in.

If you would like to find more fulfillment in your career or grow your business, join or create a mastermind group with five other people who are already successful and fulfilled in their chosen careers. Meet once a week and use that time to talk about what you've learned, your successes, and what your goals are for the coming week. Remember to share what you are grateful for as well!

THE POWER OF FIVE

Take a moment now to think about the five people you spend most of your time with and list them below. Chose an area of your life (health, career, family, relationship, etc.) and beside each name write what percentage you would rate their level of success in that particular area - (0% being not at all successful and 100% being completely successful). Once completed tally up the numbers and divide the total by five to find your projected level of success in that particular area of your life.

Name	**Level of Success**
1._____	_____%
2._____	_____%
3._____	_____%
4._____	_____%
5._____	_____%

TOTAL _____ / 5 = _____% (your level of success)

If your findings are less than exciting, change them!

Obviously there will be family members and close friends that you don't want to write out of your life. With them you may choose to just limit your topics of conversation and time spent to those areas in which they meet your desired level of success.

CLIENT RELATIONS

Challenge yourself to find something positive in every situation and you will be positively rewarded in all areas of your life. The more we share our joy by living in excellence, the more it continues to grow. With each smile, kind word or act, the energy flows over to those around us creating a ripple effect that fans out touching even more people and inspiring excellence.

Years ago I worked at a coffee shop and one of my favorite things to do was to play a game to see if I could make each customer smile before they left the store.

I especially loved a challenge and my co-workers were more than happy to leave the less than happy customers to me. Something as simple as making people smile made everyone feel great and I attracted even more wonderful things; happy customers who became new friends and kept our tip jar full, and happy employers who gave me numerous raises, let me choose my schedule, and brought me breakfast and gifts. Now, that's something to smile about!

Words give energy (vibration) to the receiver and the giver. By choosing to use words that give positive energy we are enabling ourselves and those around us to connect to our unconscious minds where we store our resources. In this state we are calm, confident and open to our channels of creativity. By putting yourself in a positive state before coming in contact with clients you will be better equipped to ensure that the outcome will be favorable to everyone. Situations that are otherwise cause for irritation are handled with ease and people who are in like states will actually be drawn to you.

▶ Put yourself in a positive state by turning your focus to all the things that you love and are excited about in your life. Remember how you felt when you were a young child and you got so excited about something you were practically vibrating? That's the feeling you want!

▶ Remember to listen to your self-talk. Even if you say and do everything correct outwardly, when you have negative thoughts on the inside, clients will pick up on the inconsistencies. They won't know exactly what you were thinking but something just won't feel right and that can be enough to cost you the sale.

▶ As you approach your customer or client, look them in the eye and smile. As you greet them, allow your smile to grow even bigger so that they feel the energy and know the smile is especially for them.

Often just being in the presence of someone who is happy is enough to make the customer smile and take them off the path of any negative vibration they came in with.

For some it takes a little more so continue to look for any way you can make them feel good as you go about your job; not just to the level of expectation but to the very best of your ability. Look for ways to surprise and impress your customers and you will be rewarded with their loyalty.

▶ Look for something you genuinely like about the person in front of you. Then compliment them sincerely on it using words that are high in positive energy such as 'beautiful', 'love', and 'thank you'.

"I love the colour of your sweater; it looks so beautiful on you."

▶ Keep your energy positive and it will carry over to your customers. Say and do the unexpected in circumstances that evoke intolerance or irritation and look for ways to place a positive spin.

For the person who held up the line to fish out exact change …

"Thank you very much; I love getting exact change, we were just about to run out."

When the person who was behind them in line approaches the counter, recognize them for their contribution...

"Hi! Thank you so much for your patience. "

▶   Go out of your way to make each person who crosses your path feel special. Treat every customer, client, co-worker, employee or boss as if they are the most important person at that moment in time.

It doesn't take much to tip the balance of someone's day toward the positive. Challenge yourself to make every person you come in contact with feel special over the next week and you will be amazed at how great you feel too! Going above and beyond in everything you do is what living in Excellence is all about and the rewards you receive are tremendous.

"...DON'T SAY ANYTHING AT ALL"

Words to live by if you can't say anything nice.

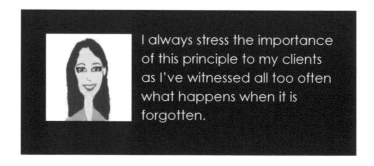

I always stress the importance of this principle to my clients as I've witnessed all too often what happens when it is forgotten.

Several years ago, two women were hired on a contract basis to help out at a fashion show. Prior to the start of the event they headed to the ladies room of the venue where the show was being held. Upon finding it silent one woman began criticizing the assistant coordinator, engaging the other woman in her plan to talk to the owner of the company and take over the assistants' position.

Their planning was cut short when the assistant came out from the bathroom stall and with only an *"Enjoy the show ladies"*, she headed out the door.

That "assistant" was a friend of mine who had invited me to watch the show that night. When the MC asked everyone to stand and recognize the CEO of the company for her tremendous contribution to the industry, it was apparent from the women's reactions that they had no idea the "assistant" they were planning to de-rail was actually the CEO. An exceptional leader who knows that the way to the top is by never getting "too good" to roll up her sleeves and do the work at the bottom.

If only those women had chosen not to say anything at all; imagine the opportunities that could have come from working with, instead of against, such an inspirational leader.

▶ Do not ever speak poorly of others. Those who do are only hurting themselves through negative vibration and the Law of Attraction. If you find yourself on the listening end of a negative conversation, put a stop to it quickly by ending it with a positive spin and then change the topic or excuse yourself from the conversation.

"Gosh, isn't it too bad about Marie?"

"Yes, but isn't it great that she is such a resourceful person? I just know that she will find a way to turn it all around."

▶ In public places such as restaurants where your conversation may easily be over heard, use discretion when speaking of others.

This applies to positive stories too! You don't know what everyone is comfortable sharing and many people are connected by only a few degrees of separation.

▶ Do not whisper in the presence of others – strangers or otherwise; if you don't want your conversation to be overheard save it for later.

If someone tells you something nice about someone else, pass it on. You will be looked upon as highly as the person who said it.

▶ Success comes not from saying how great you are but rather from being great at what you do. Real leaders don't require a title to gain respect.

▶ Be confident and modest. Do not confuse arrogance with self confidence. Arrogance is often attempting to mask insecurities while true confidence embraces humility.

▶ Speak of team effort. "We did this" not "I did that".

▶ Take responsibility if something goes wrong. Rather than stating that it wasn't your fault or passing the blame, consider how you can be part of the solution.

DO UNTO OTHERS

▶ Smile and greet all professionals where you are doing business (security, front desk, maintenance, cleaning personnel). Introduce yourself, ask their name and remember it to use on future occasions.

▶ If someone mispronounces your name, correct them right away to save them embarrassment later on.

▶ Respect others' personal space. Leave a comfortable distance between you and the other person you're engaging and pay attention to body language. If you notice them leaning or edging away, take a step back.

"What I know for sure is that what you give comes back to you."

Oprah Winfrey

▶ Choose to conduct yourself from a place of kindness and consideration at all times. Those who achieve great success and personal and professional fulfillment do so by finding opportunities to make others feel good.

The first trip to Costco with just me and my baby was a little over whelming. Being a mom was still all so new to me! While it seems like second nature now, at that time I hadn't figured out how I would manage the car seat, grocery cart, and getting the supplies into the car.

It was raining on our way in and by the time we came out of the store it had turned into a full blown storm, with high wind and torrential downpour!

As I loaded the groceries into the car, rather than let myself get frazzled, I kept imagining how wonderful it would be if the cart would just disappear so my newborn could stay dry (rather than having to take him back out of the car to return the cart), and as I lifted the last box into the car a woman came over and asked if she could take my cart for me.

Isn't it great when the Law of Attraction connects with the Rules of Etiquette?!

I was so thankful for that simple act of kindness! That was a woman living in excellence.

▶ Be aware of opportunities to help others and act on them. You will both feel good and attract more positive experiences. Something small like the offer to carry something for someone who is overloaded can shift the direction of the entire day for both of you!

▶ Send thank you cards or notes by mail for gifts, meals or other acts of kindness. Even a couple short lines expressing your appreciation are much more thoughtful than an email. Be sure to acknowledge what it is that you are thanking them for. A thank you note sent late is better than one never sent.

▶ When someone thanks you for doing something reply with a positive rather than a negative. "You're welcome" or "My pleasure" rather than "No problem."

▶ When someone gives you a compliment accept it graciously. Replying with something simple such as "Thank you very much, it's really nice of you to say." shows appreciation and confidence on your part. A compliment that is contradicted or brushed off can be enough to undermine someone's judgement and potentially keep them from wanting to give future praise.

▶ Have a single standard when it comes to how you treat people. We can't tell you how many times we have encountered people who were extremely pleasant to someone they thought 'worthy' of their time while not giving the time of day to someone they considered beneath them. You will get far better results by being consistently kind and respectful to everyone.

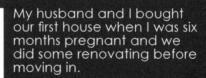

My husband and I bought our first house when I was six months pregnant and we did some renovating before moving in.

A well known furniture chain store was advertising a sale one weekend so after a morning of washing walls and without time to get cleaned up, I headed out to buy furniture while my husband started painting.

After 20 minutes in the store not one employee approached me, in fact when I made eye contact one actually looked away and walked around me to get to the well dressed couple coming through the door. Three other employees stood together looking every person up and down as they came through the entrance. It became quickly apparent that they were being very selective on whom they were going to approach.

I guess from first appearances I didn't scream big commission in my old cleaning clothes with my baby belly, hair in a ponytail and no makeup. What they didn't even take the time to find out was that I had come there that day prepared to purchase furniture for three rooms in our house.

I left there feeling a little upset and still in the need of furniture so I stopped at another store on my way home.

This time, the moment I walked in the door I heard a voice from the back of the store...

"Hi there, I will be right with you, I'm just putting on a fresh pot of coffee."

A minute later a cheerful man came and shook my hand and introduced himself as John.

He offered me coffee or water and for the next 20 minutes he showed me around the store all the while asking questions and showing genuine interest.

Had the employees at the first store approached every customer with the same kindness and professionalism they would have found out what John already knew...

John didn't just earn a commission from the furniture I purchased that day, he earned my loyalty. I have since told that story to several audiences and sent numerous family and friends to the store to ask for John, knowing that they will have an enjoyable shopping experience.

▶ You never know who your next best client will be or what they will look like. If you approach everyone with genuine curiosity you will never mistakenly let your best customer walk out the door empty handed. Successful businesses are not created by being selective with those you treat well.

▶ Be excited at the possibility of being able to help someone fulfil their needs. Be there to serve and make selling a partnership between you (the one with the product or service) and the client (the one with a vision of something you can help them achieve).

Elaborate marketing campaigns have nothing over consistent kindness; consideration to every person you encounter; that is the way to out-do the competition.

▶ Honour yourself; even if you have a fabulous person in front of you, if something doesn't feel right stick to your values and needs: it's not about being right or logical. Credit her for who she is and be okay with referring her to someone who could serve her better.

Here are a few more points to remember when it comes to Social Etiquette...

SMOKING

▶ If you must smoke don't do it in view of clients entering the building.

▶ Before going out for a smoke break put on an outer layer to help prevent smoke from clinging to your clothes.

▶ Butts are litter and contain harmful toxins. Dispose of them in a trash or cigarette can to prevent them from making way into our water systems.

▶ Wash your hands after a cigarette break and carry mints, mouth wash or a tooth brush in your purse to freshen your breath.

ELEVATOR

▶ Who ever is closest to the door exits first unless rank suggests otherwise (for example a receptionist may let the company CEO exit first).

▶ Gender is not as much of an issue when it comes to etiquette these days though the elderly and incapacitated should be given extra care.

▶ When getting in if it is already full don't cram in; wait for the next elevator.

▶ Don't ask someone to hold the door if it is closing and you aren't there yet.

▶ Once in the elevator, press the button for your floor and move to the side or back so as not to block the doors.

▶ Avoid talking on your phone, or listening to portable devices.

▶ **Escalators** – Keep to the right so that others may pass on the left.

DOORS

▶ When waiting for someone, stand against a wall and away from any doors to prevent traffic jams.

▶ The person arriving to the door first should hold it open regardless of gender.

▶ **Revolving Doors** - Don't squeeze into one already occupied. Be aware of the speed at which you go through; it affects others going through at the same time.

RUNNING LATE

▶ If you are running late, show respect and call ahead of time to notify the other party. Calling when you are supposed to be there to say you are running late is not appropriate.

▶ If you arrive late for a meeting or event, slip in discreetly with as little interruption as possible. Apologize for being late and leave it at that. Arriving in a dither and going on profusely about traffic, or what ever the excuse, causes more of a disruption to the other attendees that managed to arrive on time.

THE CAR

▶ Keep your vehicle free of clutter. Keep a box in the back to neatly contain the necessities. Include reusable bags for shopping as well as easy removal of anything that tends to accumulate.

▶ If on occasion your pet doubles as a co-pilot, be sure to keep a lint roller in your glove box to rid the seats of pet hair before anyone takes a seat. Your furry friend is the only one who should leave your car with a hairy backside!

"Dogs have owners, cats have staff."

Unknown

Telephone & Email Etiquette

"Warning: the Internet may contain traces of nuts."

Unknown

The words we use don't just have an effect when used in face to face conversation. The language we use in emails, text messages and while speaking on cellular phones have an even stronger effect on our bodies then those used in face to face conversation and hand written letters; therefore, they must be given careful consideration.

Dr. Masaru Emoto says that *"...the vibration of the human nervous system is actually on the same level as the vibration of electric communication systems such as e-mail and chat rooms. When you write something by hand or print something, the vibration is not fine enough to resonate with your nervous system, limiting the effect that the vibration can have on you. Writing involving electric fields harmonizes perfectly with the vibration of your nervous system, resulting in the formation of resonance and making it possible for an e-mail or text message to have an enormous effect on your brain and body. Normal words spoken face-to-face with no particular harmful effect can become a damaging weapon through a cell phone."*

While it's best to keep your words and thoughts positive at all times, if you have something negative you must convey then arrange a face-to-face meeting and avoid communicating it via email or on a cellular phone.

TELEPHONE

▶ Before making a call, put a smile on your face as it will change the tone of your voice and the person you are calling will hear the difference.

▶ Timing is important when making a call. In most cases calls should be placed between 9:00 am and 8:00 pm on weekdays, 10:00 am – 9:00 pm on Saturdays and 12:00 pm – 8:00 pm on Sundays.

▶ Call waiting – let the incoming call go to voice mail. If the incoming call is important answer it only to let the person know you will call them back shortly.

▶ Return calls within 24 hours from the time messages are left.

CELL PHONES

The question regarding appropriate use of cell phones for talking, texting, and surfing the net is one that we are often asked.

In some circles texting in the company of others is second nature, but in many situations people do take offense to it. In most cases it is disruptive (whether the people you are in the presence of will say so or not).

▶ Do not take calls or text while in an appointment, meeting or conference. Turn your ringer off.

▶ You will go much further in business and in personal relationships by respecting other people's time and giving them your complete attention while in their presence.

▶ If you are expecting an important call let those you are meeting with know you have been waiting for an important time-sensitive call and ask if they would mind excusing you briefly when it comes in. Turn your phone onto vibrate and when the call comes in quietly excuse yourself to another room before answering.

▶ Update your voice mail message often to notify callers that you are with clients and will be checking messages every two hours (or within a time frame appropriate for you). Make sure you follow through.

▶ If you must be on the phone in public be discrete, quick, and keep your voice low at all times. Those around you do not find your conversation impressive or charming.

▶ Whether in a store, at the checkout, or ordering food, it is disrespectful to the person serving you to have to work around your call.

▶ Avoid using cell phones in restaurants, museums, churches, theatres and washrooms.

EMAIL

"I don't believe in email. I'm an old-fashioned girl. I prefer calling and hanging up."

Sarah Jessica Parker

Email is great for transmitting information quickly over great distance and it definitely has its place. However, it doesn't replace the results of a phone call or face-to-face meeting.

While it's easy to correspond via email, it acts as a barrier between you and your emotions. Taking the time to personally speak to and visit with your customers, employees, and friends will create relationships that evoke loyalty in times when you need it most. Remember that the way to success is through building strong relationships. Move out from behind that computer screen and you'll be amazed at the doors that open up for you.

▶ Re-read emails before hitting 'send' to ensure your message is accurately conveyed and professional. Being quick does not excuse lack of courtesy.

▶ Only choose "reply all" when your reply is relevant to all parties. Be respectful of other's time by not filling up their inbox with unnecessary emails. (This includes jokes and chain mail).

▶ Avoid strong emotion in emails. If you are having a problem with someone, deal with it in person.

▶ Keep business emails short. If you have a lot to cover, call or arrange a meeting to ensure all points are addressed and nothing is over looked.

"In the time honored tradition of email, just ignore the question."

John Dobbin

Image

"Fashion can be bought. Style one must possess."

Edna Woolman Chase

Your image is your calling card! Until someone gets to know you, it is your appearance on which they will base their first impression of you. With 83% of decisions being made with our eyes, visual presentation is now the biggest selling feature of any business.

The first ten seconds of meeting someone are the most crucial. In those few seconds, we look, categorize, and decide what we believe to be true about them.

What do you want people to think about you?

Start by taking a look at what you think about yourself. No matter what you wear or how much makeup you apply, if you are critical and all you can see are the things you don't like about yourself then you'll become more like that which you don't like. When you look at yourself in a positive way and turn your focus toward the things you love, your confidence will grow and you will become even more beautiful.

WARDROBE

"His wardrobe was extensive—very extensive—not strictly classical perhaps, not quite new, nor did it contain any one garment made precisely after the fashion of any age or time, but everything was more or less spangles; and what can be prettier than spangles!"

Charles Dickens

BODY IMAGE

When it comes to wardrobe, it is important to know what will look good on us and what suits our personality. How do you **feel** in your clothes?

Looking good has a lot to do with how we feel. There is a reason why we all have favourite outfits or pieces of clothing. For some it could be because we know they look fabulous on us. Or it could be a security piece (for example, an over-sized shirt that covers your waistline and thighs). The clothes may not look flattering but we feel better thinking no one will notice our not-so-favourite body parts.

Shapeless baggy shirts hide not only your figure but your personality!

I find the biggest mistake women make is wearing clothes that are too big on them.

I always say, if you dress in a large rectangle...guess what?... You look like a large rectangle, totally defeating the purpose!

Our goal is to help you learn to accentuate the positive and fabulous things about **YOU**! To find out what looks good on you, you have to know what your best features are.

Take a moment now to write down three things you like about your physical self.

_____

_____

_____

Wear pieces that will emphasize these good points. For example if you put eye colour as one of your best features, then buy clothing in colours that will enhance the colour of your eyes. If you have blue or green eyes, wearing a top or scarf in a slightly brighter shade than your eyes will really bring out the colour.

Now if you wrote down breasts (you go girl!) but when it comes to business, unless you work at Hooters, keep it subtle.

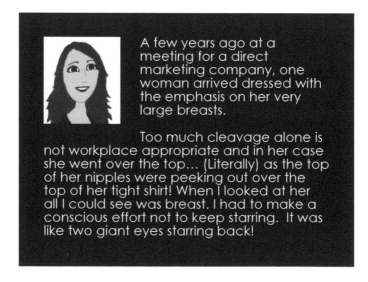

A few years ago at a meeting for a direct marketing company, one woman arrived dressed with the emphasis on her very large breasts.

Too much cleavage alone is not workplace appropriate and in her case she went over the top... (Literally) as the top of her nipples were peeking out over the top of her tight shirt! When I looked at her all I could see was breast. I had to make a conscious effort not to keep starring. It was like two giant eyes starring back!

From the comments floating around the room, I can tell you that it was not appreciated and it definitely was not in her best interest to be dressed in such a way. When you are dealing with both men and women, you want to be taken seriously not ogled or joked about. When doing business keep the breasts tucked in! Everyone around you will appreciate it.

CLOTHING

▶ Remember, this isn't the seventies. Women now have more choice then ever before on wardrobe.

▶ Have some fun and let your personality come through. Just be sure to always keep in mind the type of work you do.

If you work in industries such as law, health, banking, and finance, you will need to stay on the traditional side of business clothing. If you work in an industry that is creative such as fashion, information technology, advertising, and entertainment, you are able to show more personal style.

▶ Your clothes should be event and location appropriate.

▶ Show respect for the place and time by having your look reflect the feel of the occasion.

▶ You should be able to mix and match a majority of the items in your wardrobe.

▶ Pair your pencil skirt with a long sleeved sweater or blazer and a short- sleeved blouse with a pair of tailored pants)…

Remember: If your top is low, your legs shouldn't show!

The eye will naturally go to areas of bared skin so chose only one area to bare at a time.

▶ Keep in mind colour. Stick to neutral colours for key pieces such as jackets and pants and add colour with your tops and accessories. Many colours go well with neutrals such as dark brown, black, camel, navy, & grey.

The best time to shop for shoes is the middle to end of the day. As your day progresses, your feet get tired and swell. If you are buying a shoe for evening wear only, try them on in the evening. You and your feet will be happy dancing the night away!

▶ If you are petite, avoid chunky shoes as these throw off your proportions and it will look like you have two weights on your feet.

> A round toe high heel is very flattering for your calves.

"Funny that a pair of really nice shoes make us feel good in our heads – at the extreme opposite end of our bodies."

Levende Waters

NYLONS

▶ If you wear panty hose carry a spare pair in your purse for that inevitable run. Got a snag and no spare in the bag? Bare leg it…and hope you shaved!

▶ Sheer tights are much more flattering then opaque and give your leg some shape.

> If you are wearing a skirt and no nylons *(If this is acceptable at your workplace)* then try a nude shoe. This will create the illusion of longer legs.

"I don't know who invented the high heel, but all men owe him a lot."

Marilyn Monroe

▶ Jewelry – Stick to one or two key pieces that compliment rather than compete with each other. (Skip the noisy bracelets)

"Never wear anything that panics the cat."

P.J. O'Rourke

HERE IS A BASIC WARDROBE THAT ANY CAREER WOMAN CAN START WITH:

▶ **Selection of quality undergarments**
Before buying new clothes, buy some new underwear. There are amazingly cunning pieces to keep you tucked in. Panty lines and back bulges- be gone!

▶ **Coloured shirts/blouses**
A pretty colour or print can keep things fresh!

▶ **A tailored three piece suit in a neutral colour**
(Jacket, pant and skirt) The key being tailored. A boxy jacket will just make you look like a box. The most flattering pant is a flat-front and it flatters most midriffs. A long, wider leg is more flattering then a shorter narrow leg.

Pants should sit about one inch
from the floor with your shoes on.

▶ **White or cream cotton blouse**
A staple in any woman's wardrobe, you can wear this
with almost anything.

▶ **Sweater set**

▶ **Basic black dress**
Or a basic dress in any neutral colour. Change the look
and dress it up or down by putting a blazer or cardigan
overtop. Wear it plain and change your accessories.

▶ **Basic black pumps**

▶ **Flat dressy shoe**

"I still have my feet on the ground, I just wear better shoes."

Oprah Winfrey

Avoid shoes that cross the front of your foot. This will break the line from leg to foot and make you appear shorter.

▶ **Good quality handbag**
Be sure it has some shape! Choose a colour that will work with most of your wardrobe.

Look for shoes and handbags in similar tones, but avoid matching.

▶ **Umbrella**
Don't show up to your meeting looking like you've been put through the ringer!

WARDROBE RULES OF THUMB

▶ Clothing that fits is the number one rule! Tailored clothing is the most flattering. Make friends with a tailor in your area. Very rarely does something fit you perfectly right off the rack. If it needs to be taken in at the waist, do it. It will create curves and your waist will appear narrower.

Clothes that are too tight only magnify every flap and fold of skin. Fitted or tailored does not mean skin tight!

▶ If you have a tummy, look for pants that sit closer to your natural waistline to keep your tummy tucked in. (Your waistline is the narrowest part of your waist and is located just above your bellybutton.) Pants and jeans that sit too low will cause the tummy to spill over the top emphasizing the rolls.

A suede skirt is great to hide middle-age spread.

If you have an hourglass figure, a pencil skirt is a great way to show it off!

▶ Don't reveal too much. Avoid wearing short skirts and low cut or sheer blouses at the same time. The smart business woman knows that the key to looking authoritative and competent is to dress in a professional manner.

"A girl should be two things: classy and fabulous."

Coco Chanel

▶ Keep it pressed and clean. Nothing says unprofessional like wrinkled clothing, stains, or a ripped seam. This goes for shoes too. Avoid scuffed, dirty and over-worn shoes.

▶ Represent your company. If you are the boss, remember your employees will use you as the example. If you choose to dress casual, so will your staff.

▶ Keep trendy pieces to a minimum. Your work clothes are an investment that should last for several years. Don't let what's hot for the moment guide you when choosing your office wear. Classic quality pieces will give you timeless professionalism.

"To be a fashionable woman is to know yourself, know what you represent, and know what works for you. To be 'in fashion' could be a disaster on 90 percent of women. You are not a page out of Vogue."

Unknown

GROOMING

"Beauty is only skin deep, but ugly goes clean to the bone."

Dorothy Parker

Grooming is just as important as the clothes you wear. Taking the time to pamper yourself will make you look and feel great and your confidence will shine through.

MAKEUP

▶ Always start with clean, moisturized skin before applying makeup. This provides a smooth surface for your makeup and contributes to the overall effect.

HOMEMADE MASKS:

DRY SKIN:
Mix together a teaspoon of runny honey and a mashed, ripe avocado. Spread the mixture on your face and leave on for 15 minutes.

NORMAL SKIN:
Peel and crush cucumber to a pulp. Mix it with a teaspoon of plain yogurt and a few drops of rose water. Leave on for 15 minutes.

OILY SKIN:
Mix together a tablespoon of plain yogurt, a teaspoon of honey, a teaspoon of oatmeal and a mashed peach. Leave on for 15 minutes.

▶ Makeup should be used to enhance your features and natural beauty not to mask them.

"The best thing is to look natural, but it takes makeup to look natural."

Calvin Klein

▶ Foundation creates even skin tone and smooth texture. The perfect shade should vanish into your skin without a trace. Apply a small amount to your jaw line, cheek and forehead to ensure it matches your face and neck. Stand near a doorway or in natural light to examine the colour.

▶ To add colour to your face, smile, then lightly dust a natural colour blush to the full part of your cheeks.

▶ To create the look of more prominent cheek bones or to slim your face, make a 'fish-face' by puckering your lips and sucking in your cheeks, then apply a slightly darker blush in a curved shape in the hollows below your cheek bone.

▶ Apply concealer or foundation to your eye lids from lash to brow before applying eye shadow. This helps prevent eye shadow from creasing.

▶ You know it's time to make a change if your eye shadow receives more compliments than your eyes!

"Kiss and make up--but too much makeup has ruined many a kiss."

Mae West

▶ Usually the longer a lipstick lasts, the more drying it is to your lips.

▶ For more staying power with your lipstick, apply one coat then hold a single layer of tissue against your lips and dust on loose powder before putting on a second coat.

▶ Darker lipsticks can make you look older and lighter lipsticks, younger.

"Beauty, to me, is about being comfortable in your own skin. That, or a kick-ass red lipstick."

Gwyneth Paltrow

▶ Your eyes are one of the first features people will notice about you. They have the power to capture and communicate. Your eyebrows act as frames to your eyes, so it is important that your eyebrows are well groomed.

▶ Perfume – understated is always best.

▶ Makeup brushes should be washed at least once a month. Wash gently in warm water with a mild shampoo then rinse thoroughly. Place brushes on a clean dry towel with the hairs hanging over the edge of the counter to dry. Avoid standing them with the hairs upward which can cause water to seep into the handles and damage them.

HAIR

▶ Hair should compliment rather than upstage the rest of your look.

"I'm a big woman. I need big hair."

Aretha Franklin

Still sporting the same style you rocked ten years ago? Get out of the time warp! If you haven't received a compliment on your hair in the last three months it's time for a new 'do'!

▶ Clean, healthy hair that is kept neat and simple is always fashionable. Elaborate styles and over zealous product enhancement can go terribly wrong.

"I didn't get my hair styled today. I actually stuck my hand in a socket and this is the way it turned out."

Clinton Portis

▶ Alternate your regular shampoo with a different one every three or four washes as hair can become resistant to the ingredients.

▶ Avoid washing your hair everyday. This may cause the glands in your scalp to produce too much sebum to compensate and soon your hair will begin to look dull and greasy.

▶ Lemon juice is good for brightening blonde hair. Add four tablespoons of lemon juice to a liter of cool water and pour it over your hair, and then rinse it out.

▶ Vinegar gives dark hair extra shine. Add half a cup of vinegar to a liter of water and pour it over your hair. Rinse well.

Herbal Rinse

To make an effective herbal rinse known as an infusion, place 1 oz of your selected herb in a container and pour over 300 ml of boiling water. Soak for several hours. Strain the liquid and pour it over clean, wet hair.

▶ **Sage** leaves prevent static electricity from building up in your hair.

▶ **Marigold petals** brighten red tones in auburn hair.

▶ **Rosemary** stimulates hair growth.

In my early teens I read that Julia Roberts used mayonnaise to deep condition her hair so I decided to try it.

It was a messy procedure but I stuck it out, all the while envisioning the soft flowing locks that would follow…

Much to my dismay the result was a greasy mess! Even after four consecutive shampoos that day and several more to follow, I still had to walk around for the next week looking like I jumped into an oil slick and sporting that unforgettable 'tangy zip' scent.

I may not have got the result I wanted but I did come away with three important lessons:

1. Mayonnaise and 'sandwich spread' are not interchangeable

2. When wanting to remove an oil product add soap before the water

3. Always own at least one great hat!

"I enjoy hats and when one has filthy hair, that is a good accessory."

Julia Roberts

HANDS AND NAILS

▶ Keep hands clean and hydrated and nails neat and trimmed to equal lengths (and no chipped polish). You can't go wrong with slightly rounded nails with a natural healthy shine.

▶ Avoid hang nails by keeping your hands moisturized. For a deep moisturizing treatment, use cuticle oil regularly. Olive oil right out of your kitchen works great!

▶ Use an acetone-free nail polish remover. The acetone can dry out your fingernails.

▶ New water-based nail polishes are better for you and the environment.

"There was something in my back, I felt it. And sure enough, A pressed-on finger nail had worked itself all the way through my clothes. It was lodged in my back."

Zac Efron

Dining Etiquette

"*Ponder well on this point: the pleasant hours of our life are all connected by a more or less tangible link, with some memory of the table.*"

Charles Pierre Monselet (1825-1888)

ETIQUETTE AT THE TABLE

Over the years of teaching and speaking on matters of etiquette, dining is perhaps one of the most common areas of uncertainty amongst those we have met.

When is it okay to start eating? Is shrimp a finger food? Which plate is my bread plate? ...

Do we have some stories we could tell you!

Here's one that always comes to mind whenever the subject of dining or table etiquette comes up...

Salad fork, Dinner fork, Dessert fork...Manicure fork?

We have seen many a misused fork but this one 'nailed' it!

At a black-tie dinner event with a few hundred attendees, we were seated around tables formally set for eight. Introductions were made and as everyone acquainted themselves with one another the question as to professions was posed.

As often happens when people discover the presence of an "Etiquette Guru" (as a friend of mine fondly termed me) questions on proper conduct began. It wasn't at all out of the ordinary when the woman next to me asked which the salad fork was, and happy to help I pointed it out.

"Thank you." she said, picking up the fork.

"These fake nails are bugging me." (As she began loosening her nails with the fork)

I must not have masked my surprise well as upon looking up she was quick to reassure me...

"Oh, its okay," She said. *"I'm allergic to the dressing so I'm not going to eat the salad".*

And on that note....

Let's start with cutlery!

CUTLERY

▶   Always start from the outside piece of cutlery and work your way in towards your plate.

▶   If a salad comes first, use the fork furthest from your plate. Keep in mind the salad fork is smaller then the dinner fork (and apparently quite useful for removing acrylic nails!)

▶   The salad is not necessarily served first. During a formal dinner, salad may be served after the entrée in the European manner.

▶   The dessert utensils are often placed horizontally above the dinner plate. Dessert can be eaten with a spoon or fork.

▶   Never rest cutlery you have been using directly on the table.

CUTTING YOUR FOOD

▶   Hold your knife with your index finger pressed on the top of the knife where the handle meets the blade. Hold the fork with your index finger pressing the base of the handle with the tines down. Be sure to keep your elbows just above table level.

▶ If you are in the midst of a meal and rest your cutlery momentarily on your plate, place them in the 5 o'clock & 7 o'clock position on your plate.

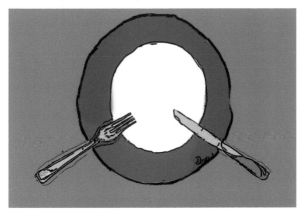

Place fork tines down.

▶ When you are done your meal, place both your knife and fork at the 3 or 9 o'clock position with the knife blade facing inward.

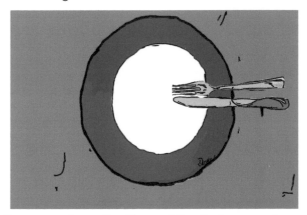

You can place the tines of the fork up or down.

PLACE SETTING

First we'll look at where everything is located on the table.

This is also helpful for setting the table properly when you are entertaining in your home.

▶ The plate and cutlery should be placed ½ inch to 1 inch from the edge of the table.

▶ There should be one foot distance between place settings.

▶ When using patterned dishes, ensure all patterns face the same direction.

▶ Forks are located to the left of the plate, the soup spoon and knife to the right side with the knife blade facing toward the plate.

▶ When setting the table remember the rule of arranging cullery according to the order courses will be served: begin from the outside and work in.

▶ The bread plate is located above the forks to the left of the plate. The butter knife is placed horizontally across the bread plate with the blade of the knife facing downward.

▶ The salad plate is located to the left of the forks.

▶ The water glass is located above and to the right of the dinner plate. The cup & saucer is to the right of the water glass.

▶ When setting the table, place the napkin to the left of the plate.

▶ Seat guests alternating male/female around the table, and always serve your guests first.

NAPKINS

▶ Wait until your host is seated and has lifted his or her napkin before placing yours on your lap.

▶ At lunch completely open your napkin and place it on your lap.

▶ For dinner where the napkins are larger, fold them in half before placing on your lap.

▶ Do not use a cloth napkin to blot your lipstick. Do use it to blot food from your face from time to time as needed during the meal.

▶ If you get up from the table during the meal, leave your napkin on the seat or arm of your chair.

▶ The table should be a "napkin free zone" until everyone has finished eating and the host places her napkin on the table signaling the meal is finished. If the plates have been cleared place your napkin directly in front of you, otherwise to the left or right of your plate is acceptable. Do not refold it but do place it neatly rather than in a ball.

We thought this might be too obvious to add, but then looking back over some of our experiences perhaps one woman's "obvious" is another's next faux pas - so here it goes...

▶ Never use your napkin as a tissue, and never blow your nose at the table!

SOUP

▶ Crush crackers that come in individual packages while the package is still sealed then open over your soup.

▶ When eating soup, spoon away from you allowing for the soup to cool and drip in the bowl rather than your lap. Eat from the side of the spoon.

A little ditty by Pelteson to help you remember...

"As a ship sails out to sea, I spoon my soup away from me."

I make this technique fun for my kids by singing it to them.

▶ Avoid hunching over the bowl and don't slurp your soup. (Except when in Japan and some other Asian countries where slurping your soup is considered a compliment to the chef!)

BREAD ROLL

I was at a women's networking event at a sit-down dinner. Our meal was served and as the buns came around the woman seated to my right used the correct bread plate, however, the woman to my left had used the wrong one leaving me without. Well, not wanting to embarrass anyone I ended up putting my bun on top of my salad. (It was that or on top of the chicken with sauce.) The bun stood out like a giant mountain erupting from a forest and my plate looked twice the size of everyone else's!

As in this case, using the wrong bread plate probably won't be something your client or associate will point out. Just know it isn't looked highly upon, especially if the person next to you is stuck without one...and knows the etiquette rules!

▶ When eating bread or a dinner roll, use your fingers to break the bread into pieces small enough for 1 or 2 bites. Do not use a knife to cut your bread roll.

▶ Butter pieces one at a time just prior to eating them, rather than buttering the entire roll or slice all at once.

DURING THE MEAL

▶ Maintain good posture during the meal, and keep elbows off the table once the food has arrived. Before and after the meal, leaning in on your elbows is acceptable and creates a more intimate setting for conversation.

▶ Pass food around the table counter clockwise.

▶ When someone asks for the salt, always pass both salt and pepper together.

▶ Eat quietly and take small bites. If someone asks you a question you will be able to finish that bite and respond much quicker than if you have chipmunk cheeks worth of food to get down.

▶ Refrain from adding salt or bottled sauces to your food until you have tasted it. It may insult the chef to assume that it is not well seasoned. After your first bite, feel free to use as much salt as required or your arteries can tolerate!

▶ When eating meat, cut one piece at a time. Do not cut up the entire piece at once (unless it's for your four year old).

▶ Mop up that last bit of sauce from your plate by putting a small piece of bread on the end of your fork to soak it up. Do not hold the bread in your fingers to wipe the plate.

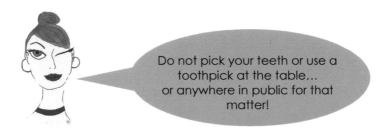

CHALLENGING FOOD

▶ Some foods require more effort to eat gracefully than others. When out for a business meal (or first date, or anytime impressions are important) go for foods that are easier to eat and save your focus for the conversation rather than on twirling your linguine.

Some foods best avoided are crab, lobster, and fish with bones, unpeeled shrimp, olives (or anything with pits), long pastas, and messy burgers.

▶ Condiments - Never dip your food directly into a condiment dish that is set out for the entire table. Instead, spoon a small portion onto the edge of your plate. Ketchup should also be placed on the side of your plate. Dip pieces of food into it one piece at a time.

THAT LEFT A BAD TASTE!

Now say you just ate something bad that must be removed from your mouth, what would you do?

While at a lunch meeting an associate had the displeasure of biting into something she found unpleasant...

After a loud *"Ewww!"* attracting the attention of everyone around the table, she proceeded to announce (with her mouth full)...

"Look out I'm going to do something gross."

She then leaned forward, opened her mouth and allowed the offending bite to roll out of her mouth and onto her plate!

"Excuse me Sir, can we get another sandwich for my colleague here... with a side of etiquette please?"

▶ Discretion is the key! Unless you have something in your mouth that won't go down without coming back up, take a sip of your beverage to mask the taste and muster the strength to get it down. Otherwise simply move the offending morsel forward with your tongue, onto your fork, and place it discretely on the side of your plate.

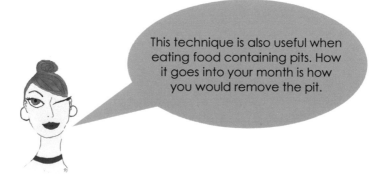

This technique is also useful when eating food containing pits. How it goes into your month is how you would remove the pit.

WHAT DO YOU DO IF...

▶ **Someone at your table spills a drink?**

The more calm and unfazed you remain the better you will look and they will feel. By gasping "oh no!" and stopping all conversation to look over only draws more attention to the situation. If you were in the midst of a conversation simply pass them your napkin as you continue talking. The more you can move the focus to something else the greater their appreciation for allowing them to recover gracefully.

▶ **You have been invited out for dinner with the boss or client?**

Do not order alcohol unless they do, and limit it to one. The last thing you need is to be fumbling on your words and stumbling out of the restaurant!

▶ **You find a fly in your soup or a bug in your salad?**

"Please keep it down or everyone might want one." Don't make a big deal if you find something unwanted in your meal. If you are at a restaurant and make the discovery near the beginning of the meal it is acceptable to discreetly ask the wait staff for another dish, if you can do so without disruption. When at someone's home just leave that particular dish on your plate and eat everything else. Do not embarrass your host by calling attention to it.

CORPORATE EVENTS

▶ When at a corporate event, keep the alcohol to a minimum.

 Believe me, I'm all for a drink or two, (well anything with vodka really) but please do not drown your common sense with a few too many cocktails or you just may end up doing something you will regret.

At my husband's Christmas party last year I witnessed a perfect example of just that...

One female employee, obviously a little too into the holiday "spirits", got carried away and was on the dance floor grinding and rubbing up against every male that would have it...and right next to the president of the company who is female!

Not the way to get a promotion!

Unless your goal is to be the subject of talk around the water cooler for the next month you may want to stick to punch for the greater part of the evening...just be sure to check that it wasn't spiked!

Remember: Just because an event takes place outside of regular office hours and in a relaxed atmosphere doesn't mean that what you do and how you behave won't be noted.

HORS D'OEUVRES

▶ If hors d'oeuvres are being passed around on a tray by wait staff, take a napkin from the tray and hold it in your hand for as long as you intend to enjoy the food. If you have a plate hold the napkin under the plate.

▶ Do not bring the food directly from the tray to your mouth. Take it from the tray to your napkin or plate then pick it up to eat it.

▶ Avoid eating, talking, and drinking all at the same time unless you own shares in stain remover pens.

"Your Business clothes are naturally attracted to staining liquids. This attraction is strongest just before an important meeting."

Scott Adams

▶ If you are left with toothpicks or skewers from hors-d'oeuvres, hold the toothpick in your napkin until you find a waste basket. Sometimes the wait staff will have a small receptacle on their tray for used toothpicks.

▶ Always use a napkin to wipe your fingers. Do not lick your fingers as tempting as that last bit of chocolate may be!

A FEW MORE POINTS WORTH MENTIONING...

▶ Purses and bags don't belong on the table.

▶ The host of a meal (the person who invited the other) should pay regardless of the gender of the host or that of the other parties.

▶ In business, the person who potentially would gain more from the meeting should pay regardless of who did the inviting.

▶ If co-workers go for lunch it is acceptable for them to split the bill or ask for separate bills.

▶ At a buffet, when going back for seconds, take a new plate rather then carrying your used plate back for reloading.

▶ Never run your fingers through your hair or comb your hair at the table.

▶ Cutlery should not double as a mirror and lipstick should not be applied at the table.

▶ Excuse yourself from the table and leave the broccoli removal and makeup application for the ladies room.

▶ At times, subtle use of lip balm is acceptable at the table – use your discretion.

▶ Unfortunately when it comes to lipstick and dining, the "stick" ends up less on the lips and more on the cups, glasses and napkins.

Avoid leaving a trail of your glossy glow by discretely moistening your lips before you take a sip to prevent the transfer. This technique works even better if you can moisten the rim of your glass too. *(For those of you who just got an image of a horse at the salt block, we do not condone licking your glass...No, not even on the sugary rims of your margaritas.)* Instead, as you reach for your glass use your thumb to gently lift some of the condensation from the outside up to the rim.

A Virginia proverb reminds us,

"One cannot think well, love well and sleep well when one has not dined well."

Etiquette at Home

The Home Office

"*Organize your life around your dreams – and watch them come true.*"

Unknown

HOME OFFICE

I t used to be that those of us working from home were not taken as seriously as those who work from an outside office. We really believe that this is starting to change.

Clients care about quality of service and a positive experience more than the flash of an expensive office. Business owners who have less overhead often have less stress and more money and time to put towards better pricing and personal touches.

People from all backgrounds and types of businesses are leaving the corporate world and starting up on their own. They are getting smarter with their time and focusing on what really matters to them.

We've seen amazing things done from home offices!

I have my office in my home and I wouldn't have it any other way. I think one of the best reasons is that it allows me the freedom to control my time...which is also one of the biggest downfalls!

My home office, even though it is the size of a school locker (and I'm not kidding, I took my daughters closet) enables me to be with my children. I am the one to pick them up from school and have the flexibility to go to functions and activities. I get the best of both worlds.

Achieving personal and professional excellence isn't always as easy as we would like, especially when the boarders between the two become muddied. Having an office at home allows for great freedoms and it also opens up the possibility of crossing areas of our lives causing one to take time away from another. Setting clear boundaries that enable you to keep aligned with your values is an important and often overlooked step.

While for some it's all too easy to let the dishes and the laundry take priority when working from home, it's just as easy for others to spend hours on the computer, missing irreplaceable time with their families and causing relationships to suffer.

Take a look at your values and determine what is most important to you. Usually where you spend a majority of your time is what you value the most. During different periods of our lives our values will change, often following major events such as becoming a parent, or experiencing a health scare.

Having an ultra-successful career loses its value when you don't have anyone to share it with or you are too ill to enjoy the lifestyle it provides.

If at this point in your life 'career' is your highest value, you will likely want to dedicate the largest allotment of time toward that area. Just be sure to still allow sufficient time to the other areas to maintain a balance that is appropriate for you.

▶ Take some time to check in on how you feel about each area of your life (health and fitness, family and relationships, personal development, spirituality, and career). If what you are doing looks good on the surface but doesn't feel good, then it isn't in alignment with your values. Remember to check in with how you are feeling and make any adjustments necessary to get back in alignment.

On the following page are some things to consider when having a home office along with tips to making it a viable situation if you are thinking of either starting a business or moving your office home.

BENEFITS

Financial

▶ Working from home can lower your monthly overhead by eliminating costly lease or rent payments on office space.

▶ You will be more likely to eat lunch at home which is cost effective and allows for healthier options.

▶ Travel expenses for fuel and vehicle maintenance are reduced considerably.

▶ You may have a reduced car insurance premium.

▶ It is more environmentally friendly!

▶ The money you save from overhead can go into marketing or other aspects of your business. You decide where your dollars are best allocated.

▶ There can also be some great tax benefits to working from home.

Freedom

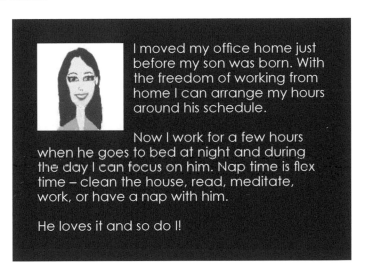

I moved my office home just before my son was born. With the freedom of working from home I can arrange my hours around his schedule.

Now I work for a few hours when he goes to bed at night and during the day I can focus on him. Nap time is flex time – clean the house, read, meditate, work, or have a nap with him.

He loves it and so do I!

▶ By working from home you have the freedom to take your business in any direction you feel fit. You can operate it and change directions with it as you feel necessary. Knowing this allows the creativity to flow anytime day or night!

Comfort

▶ Lets face it, there is nothing like walking to work in your pyjamas! You save time and energy not having to deal with long commutes to work. The office gossip and a boss looking over your shoulder is no longer an issue. You are the one who plans your day, your time, and your schedule!

OVERCOMING CHALLENGES

While there are many benefits to working from home there are a few things to be aware of as well.

Discipline

▶ Discipline plays a large part in success. It's not always as easy as you would like to get work done when you see dirty dishes in the sink, the kids and dog want attention and piles of laundry are screaming your name. Trying to decide what to make a priority can drive you crazy at times if you let it. Create a schedule in accordance to your values and let it be your guide.

▶ For some the discipline issue can go the other way too. Be sure that having your office at home doesn't end up meaning you are "always at work." Set office hours and let your phone go to voice mail outside of those times so as not to take away from family and leisure time.

Cook in batches and freeze. This allows you to just pull something healthy from the freezer and it's ready in no time.

Allocating the right amount of time to all areas of life can sometimes be tricky especially when one gets really focused on growing a business.

This was something that took me some time to 'get'. It wasn't until I was witnessing the negative effect not only on myself, but my family, that I realized it was important to make some changes.

My solution was to forget about the house until 4:30 pm, and then switch into domestic mode; making dinner, cleaning, helping with homework and so forth. It's amazing what you can get done in a short amount of time when you are focused. The rest of the evening I spend with my husband and children. I found that once I was able to switch off work, life became more peaceful and everyone was happier!

Balance

▶ If you like the idea of a home office but don't want to have clients coming to your home you can find offices that you rent by the hour/day at reasonable rates. This will allow you to see clients in a professional setting, while still doing a majority of the work from home. Book all your appointments in one or two days, allowing you to free your time for the rest of the week.

I actually have a rental space that I use when meeting clients and running programs and classes.

This allows me work from home on days when I don't have clients and I can keep my home office just for me! (After all, it is just a closet!)

Details

▶ You are forced to deal with everything when you are self-employed. You are responsible for all aspects of your business, including the tasks you find tedious. Just because you work from home does not mean you have to be a one woman show!

I have three subcontractors who all work from their home offices, one of whom lives 900 kilometers away. The flexibility is great!

Moving the office home was the best thing for my business. I now rent an office in a business centre on an as-needed basis when meeting with clients and utilize the full time reception services there to collect our mail and deliveries. It enabled me to use the money that had been allocated for rent to hire employees and now I can dedicate my time towards what I enjoy; being with my family, and creating new ways of growing the company which benefits everyone.

▶ Hire someone to help you with the areas that are not your areas of expertise or you have no interest in. This allows you to focus on what you are good at and really maximizes the growth potential of your business. If the money to hire someone is not there in the beginning consider trading services.

> Hire a housekeeper to come to your home once or twice a month to take care of the bigger cleaning jobs; use that extra time for income generating activities.

Learn to say No

▶ Don't let friends and family convince you to take on any extra responsibilities, assuming since you're home, you must have extra time.

▶ Let family and friends know when you are working and when is a good time to drop by for a visit.

Isolation

▶ Isolation can be a problem when working from home. Join a women's networking group or mastermind group with other entrepreneurs. This will allow you to get out and talk to others and stay connected. Not only will this keep you sane, it will allow you to get different ideas and thoughts on improving your business. It is almost impossible to grow a business alone!

Taking Calls

▶ This can be a challenge when you have a child at home.

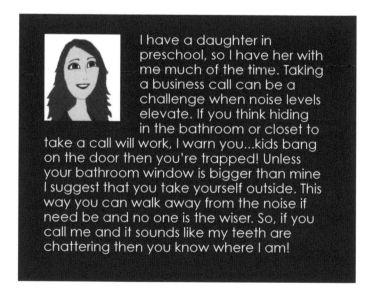

I have a daughter in preschool, so I have her with me much of the time. Taking a business call can be a challenge when noise levels elevate. If you think hiding in the bathroom or closet to take a call will work, I warn you...kids bang on the door then you're trapped! Unless your bathroom window is bigger than mine I suggest that you take yourself outside. This way you can walk away from the noise if need be and no one is the wiser. So, if you call me and it sounds like my teeth are chattering then you know where I am!

▶ Don't pick up a business call if there is chaos around you. It is much better to let it go to voice mail than to answer when you won't be at your best.

"Organizing is what you do before you do something, so that when you do it, it is not all mixed up."

A. A. Milne

KIBBLES AND TIDBITS

"Dogs come when they're called; cats take a message and get back to you later."

Mary Bly

▶ When bringing clients to your home keep pets in the back yard or in a room that is closed off from the area where you do business.

▶ Unless you are in the pet industry, remove all accessories and signs of pet hair. Not everyone is a pet lover and even those who are may not appreciate Fifi's hair on their suit or a parrot flying around their head.

"Home office professionals should be applauded. They demonstrate a great amount of initiative, ambition and perseverance..."

Tracey Crockett

99

International Etiquette

"When you travel, remember that a foreign country is not designed to make you comfortable. It is designed to make its own people comfortable."

Clifton Fadiman (1904 - 1999)

Our perception is learned and sets limltations for us. If you put flies in a jar with a lid on it and over time you remove the lid they won't fly out of the jar. (Yes, the lid had holes for air.) Fish in a tank with a piece of glass down the middle won't use the other half of the tank once the glass is removed.

Why?

The neurology wasn't developed. They would have to create new neurological connections in order to broaden their reality and have the perception that something else is possible.

We freeze our perception in time and when we open ourselves up to the perception that something is possible we unfreeze it. We create new neuro-networks and then find ourselves able to see there is a whole new world of opportunity.

What's outside of the lid on your jar or on the other side of your tank?

101

Changing your perception can be as simple as looking at your situation from someone else's point of view. (Close your eyes and put your self in another person's shoes and look back at yourself through their eyes.) Then look at yourself and your current situations from the perspective of an impartial fly on the wall, simply observing.

How have you been limiting youself?
Where have you set your own glass ceiling?
Would you like to expand your business? Earn more? Travel more? ...

If something is possible in the world then it is possible for you and those around you!

Do I hear international travel anyone?

Before taking your work outside of your country it is important to take the time to learn about the people you intend to meet and their role within the company. Knowing the traditions and expectations of the country you are travelling to will ensure you are well received.

There are entire books written on how to do business with specific countries. Here we will give you some brief and important points to keep in mind when travelling internationally on business.

▶ Today English is spoken in most parts of the world. However, don't let this fool you into thinking you don't need to know any of the native language. Your effort will be appreciated even if your accent isn't perfect. Learning greetings and a few common words and sentences will go a long way to creating rapport and a positive impression with your hosts.

▶ Know what your body language is saying. When in another country certain gestures may have a very different meaning than what you think you are portraying.

Avoid the 'OK' sign (making a circle with your thumb and index finger). **In Japan this is considered obscene.**

HANDSHAKES & GREETINGS

▶ In North America and Europe a firm handshake is acceptable and preferred.

▶ In the Middle East and Asia, the handshake is gentler. A very firm handshake can signal aggression.

▶ Shaking hands with women is acceptable and expected. The exception is in Islamic countries were it is considered offensive.

In many countries standing with your hands on your hips signals aggression.

Japan

▶ The bow is equivalent to the handshake. Rank is very important, so keep in mind the person with the inferior rank is to bow first. If you are there to meet an important client, you should bow first to show respect. They will state their company first, then their name.

China

▶ A slight bow of the head and a handshake is appropriate. Be sure to lower your eyes to show respect.

▶ Address people by their title or position first and then their last name.

▶ When it comes to business, women are still considered

second class citizens. However, coming from North America, you shouldn't have any problems as long as you are dressed conservatively.

In North America, eye contact shows that you are listening and that you are giving someone your attention. In some Asian countries, eye contact is regarded as impolite.

Philippines

▶ Business people will greet you with a handshake and eye contact. Keep in mind that men may not initiate a handshake with women.

India

▶ In the Westernized parts of India, business people will shake hands with a slight bow of the head or nod. In the more traditional areas the men will not touch women outside of their families; instead they will bow with palms together.

PERSONAL SPACE

▶ **In North America and Europe** maintaining two or three feet of personal space between you and the person you are speaking with is acceptable.

▶ **In Japan and other Asian countries,** they require more space, so be careful not to get too close. As for many of the other countries, they often like to get closer.

DRESS CODE

▶ Before going into another country it is important to do your research and respect their dress code. For business, stay to the conservative side by wearing tops with sleeves and avoid low necklines.

▶ Avoid jewellery in excess and pieces of a religious nature.

▶ Keep makeup natural.

BUSINESS CARDS

China

Have business cards
that are bilingual and
with the Chinese
lettering in black or gold.

> **Reminder:**
>
> As stated earlier, avoid putting a business card in your back pocket especially when in Asian countries as this is considered disrespectful; use your jacket pocket instead.

Japan

Business cards should be in
both English and Japanese.
Present your card with two
hands, with the Japanese side up facing your recipient.

Germany

Business cards that have university degrees and honours are
looked at positively.

Spain

Have cards printed in both English and Spanish and present
it with the Spanish side facing your recipient.
**Refer to CONVERSATIONAL ETIQUETTE for more on business
cards.**

"Why buy good luggage? You only use it when you travel."

Yogi Berra

Executive
Etiquette

"The difference between a boss and a leader: a boss says, 'Go!' -a leader says, 'Let's go!'"

E. M. Kelly

LEADERSHIP

"If everyone would sweep their own doorstep, the whole world will be clean."

Mother Teresa

We are all born to lead. It isn't a degree, a position or a fancy office that makes a leader. A leader is someone who lives in excellence personally and professionally, expressing her best, no matter what the position or role, not just at work but in every area of life. In doing so she lifts her life and the lives of everyone she meets. She is in alignment with her core values, doors begin to open and amazing opportunities naturally follow the stream of energy.

Excellence and Leadership come before every success and every great accomplishment. In fact, this section of the book could easily have been called 'Excellence' as Leadership and Excellence truly go hand-in-hand.

"Most people who want to get ahead do it backward. They think, 'I'll get a bigger job, then I'll learn how to be a leader.' But showing leadership skill is how you get the bigger job in the first place. Leadership isn't a position, it's a process."

John Maxwell

Excellence isn't something that is achieved over night. It is the accumulation of small consistent steps that move us forward towards our desired outcome. This starts a chain reaction, momentum that will propel us onward with increasing ease to be a model of leadership in our relationships, with our health, spirituality, finances, personal development, and our careers.

To be a leader means to have a genuine desire to make a positive difference. Before we can lead anyone else we must be able to lead ourselves and it starts with the genuine desire to do everything we do to the best of our ability and to always have an excellent attitude.

Before there was a great leader, there was a great person living in excellence. The first step to becoming a leader is to take personal responsibility for our current situation rather than assigning blame to those around us. Once we acknowledge that we are 100% responsible for everything that goes on in our lives we have the power to create any reality we desire.

Begin each day with the intention that you will give everything, do everything, and be everything necessary to be the catalyst that raises the level of service, to go above and beyond the level of expectation bringing joy to self and others.

▶ Support and inspire everyone to demonstrate leadership (excellence) in their current roles personally and professionally; friend, wife, mother, entry level file clerk to the CEO. For any establishment to truly succeed each person must be demonstrating excellence.

▶ Employers and managers who set a standard of expectation through example with their own conduct will inspire employees to follow.

▶ Invest in people, build them up and allow them opportunities to shine.

▶ Put your time and focus only on the things you do very well rather than spreading yourself thin trying to do everything alone. Do fewer things and do them better by hiring people who naturally excel in areas you don't.

▶ Lead your team with encouragement rather than using your authority to instill fear.

▶ Always be willing to personally do any task you ask of your staff. Don't impose rules or expectations on your employees that you don't follow.

"Insecure leaders are always positioning themselves to look good in the eyes of others. Insecure leaders are more concerned with how they look than how their people look, and that spells trouble."

John Maxwell

▶ Speak in terms of what your team accomplished rather than what 'you' did. If you claim the glory for the work others did you are likely to be resented. Give recognition and praise to your team and they will out shine themselves time and time again.

EMPLOYER/EMPLOYEE RELATIONSHIP

"Asking 'who ought to be the boss?' is like asking' who ought to be the tenor in the quartet?' Obviously, the man who can sing tenor."

Henry Ford

The relationship between employers and employees is a two way street. As employers we play a significant role in ensuring the success of our employees and our companies through our language, actions, behaviors, attitude and example. People who are treated with respect and kindness will like their job more and will be loyal and efficient. Loyal and efficient employees will treat their employers, co-workers and clients with kindness and respect.

Hold the duality of accepting who your employees are while holding the vision of their potential rather than judging them first then holding the potential.

"A good boss makes his men realize they have more ability than they think they have so that they consistently do better work than they thought they could."

Charles Erwin Wilson

▶ A pay cheque is not always enough, nor is it the only way in which to compensate employees. Allowing your team the flexibility to incorporate family and leisure time, personal activities, telecommunicating from home, and flexible hours are of great asset to everyone.

▶ When a job is well done, give the employee the praise she deserves, mentioning one or two specific things that were done well. Most people will work harder for recognition than they will for wages alone. For owners of small businesses on a tight budget, praise may be the only reward they can afford; accordingly, that makes the praise and compliments all the more important!

▶ Varying the way in which compliments are delivered is beneficial (over the phone, in person, email, or written letter or card). Written letters of praise and congratulations show your appreciation and may be kept for professional portfolios.

▶ Motivate employees and co-workers through compliments that make them feel good rather than creating pressure. Mini compliments such as "You tried hard" send a message of encouragement whereas expressions such as "Keep at it" "Try harder" (while meaning well) do not have the same motivational impact.

▶ Being someone's boss doesn't mean being bossy. Use uplifting words when speaking with your team to positively influence their state as well as your own.

▶ **Suggestion Sandwich** - When you would like someone to do something differently sandwich suggestions with compliments.

1. First compliment them overall on **the big picture** (on their performance, work ethic, presentation or whatever the case may be).

   "Jill, you've had a great month. The sales are up and your enthusiasm for the job is so wonderful to see."

2. The second layer should be a compliment on a specific thing they did well.

   "I especially loved that you took the time to really get to know your clients and prearranged to have a special meal alternative available for Mrs. Granger."

3. Lastly end with what you would like to see done differently and **word it in the positive**.

   "What would make next month <u>even</u> better is following up each appointment with a personal note to thank them for their time and let them know how much you enjoyed getting to know them."

▶ Word it in the positive; tell people what you want, not what you don't want. When someone hears what you don't want them to do they have to make a picture of it in their mind to process it. Then that image is what is in their mind and they still don't know what you want them to do.

What's the first thing someone does when you say, "Don't look over there." – They look!
If you say, "Keep looking this way." – They will.

Instead of saying, "Don't forget to post the invoices before you leave today." Say "please _remember_ to post the invoices before you leave today."

▶ Make sure employees are clear on what is expected of them whether it is written down or conveyed and reinforced in your day-to-day interaction.

▶ Be clear as to your expectations when setting standards in the area of ethics and job performance.

Ethics will ensure your staff are representing you and the company appropriately in the daily dealings and will help them when faced with decisions.

You will increase your company's productivity and profits by being specific with your expectations regarding job performance.

▶ When dealing with offenses to ethical standards, it is your role as the employer or manager to help guide them back to the right path. Handle the situation with dignity by sitting down with your employee and having a sincere conversation on how to rectify the problem.

▶ Listen to what they have to say, and stay calm while making it clear that what they did was against company policy and must not be done again. When appropriate, you may also point out that a future occurrence would be grounds for termination.

▶ When dealing with job performance standards, develop a way in which to measure whatever productivity is required to satisfy the needs of the company's bottom line.

▶ Have employees participate in setting company goals. People will strive to achieve a goal that they are aligned with, whereas enforcing your goals on them will do little to inspire productivity.

▶ Base goals on specific numbers or quantities with timelines attached for measurability.

"People rarely succeed unless they have fun in what they are doing."

Andrew Carnegie

OUTLINE FOR PERFORMANCE REVIEWS:

▶ Set performance reviews annually or quarterly depending on the needs of your company.

▶ Keep the setting comfortable such as over coffee where you are on equal ground. In your office with your desk between you and your employee can be intimidating.

▶ Speak with your employees not to them.

▶ Begin with social conversation to get in rapport and set the tone. Then open the review by going over areas they are excelling at, giving specific examples.

▶ Next, ask them if they feel there are any areas in which they could improve. Listen to what they have to say then ask them what they think they could do to make the improvement.

▶ Then cover any other areas where you see a potential for improvement. First ask your employees for ways they can think of to change their outcomes, then offer suggestions to them. (Refer to 'Suggestion Sandwiches' under EMPLOYEE/EMPLOYER RELATIONSHIP).

▶ Don't over look any weaknesses and be tactful when covering them so as to build, rather than undermine their confidence.

▶ Make sure they are clear on your expectations. What will happen if they don't succeed in meeting the expectations? What will happen if they do? Let them know specifically what needs to happen in order for you to know the expectations have been met.

▶ Set an appropriate amount of time for the success strategies to be implemented and arrange to meet again to assess the progress at that point.

▶ Allow time for any questions and suggestions that your employee may have pertaining to the company.

POLICIES AND PROCEDURES MANUAL

Setting up a policies and procedures manual can help to eliminate confusion and misunderstandings. The following are examples of what could be included:

▶ **Company history:**

- When the company was founded and by whom

- Chart of company growth

▶ **Mission Statement/Purpose**

- The company's ethics and intentions of quality (concise and to the point)

▶ **Company Set Up**

- Outlines the departments, job levels and responsibilities of everyone

- Hiring and termination procedures

- Salary terms and compensation

- Eligibility for benefits, vacation time, and sick leave, extended medical leaves of absence and parental flextime programs, company insurance plans, options such as profit sharing, tuition reimbursements for continuing education and so on.

- Business expenses – (which job levels are eligible and details for reimbursement)

▶ **Principles of Conduct:**

- Standards for behaviour, ethics, and job performance

- Miscellaneous office policies; media relations, office security, office supplies and equipment

- Smoking, food and beverages, professional appearance including dress (dress code can be based on customer expectations.)

"I've always found that the speed of the boss is the speed of the team."

Lee Iacocca

WORKPLACE COURTESIES

"The first thing a new employee should do on the job is learn to recognize his boss' voice on the phone."

Martin Buxbaum

▶ The look of your place of business and the manner in which your employees greet clients and guests set the tone for the first impression. Keep your surroundings tidy and be sure everyone is greeted warmly and made to feel welcome. Clients don't care if you are having a bad day; they want to feel special and have the best experience getting what ever product or service they came to you for.

▶ Stand to greet someone who comes into your office & shake hands in greeting and parting.

▶ Common courtesies such as 'please' and 'thank you' are often over looked and can make all the difference. They should be remembered and used when speaking with anyone whether they are employees, wait staff at a restaurant, or management.

▶ Be specific with your thanks... Rather than just saying "Thank you", remember to add on what you are thanking them for.

   "Thank you for taking the time to organize all the bills for today's deposit. I really appreciate your attention to detail."

▶ A brief thank you note is an appropriate gesture when someone goes above and beyond for you.

▶ Tell the truth – whether you are in an entry level position, mid management or a company CEO it is far more beneficial than getting caught in a deception. Owning up to your mistakes shows confidence and is admirable. People are forgiving and they will remember a deception for a long time. Accepting responsibility is far more respected than saying *"It's not my fault!"*

"Do the one thing you think you cannot do. Fail at it. Try again. Do better the second time. The only people who never tumble are those who never mount the high wire. This is your moment. Own it."

Oprah Winfrey

AT A MEETING

▶ Plan to arrive a few minutes early to allow time to settle in without disruption.

▶ Introduce yourself to anyone you don't know and make small talk before the meeting begins.

▶ Be conscious of your posture and body language and be attentive to the speaker.

▶ If you have something to add, wait until there is a pause in conversation. Don't cut someone off and interrupt them while they are still speaking.

OFFICE GIFT GIVING

▶ Gift giving to clients, employees and bosses should be carefully considered first as depending on the industry, can be misconstrued. Gifts from employers to employees should be token gifts of thanks that reflect the amount of time the employee has been with the company. Over-expensive or personal gifts are not appropriate. Keep their interests in mind.

▶ Employees should check with their employers regarding company gift-giving policies before purchasing gifts for clients. A card with a simple message of thanks and appreciation is better received than a gift that could be misinterpreted.

▶ Downplay the opportunity to advertise with holiday gifts to clients. Gifts that bare a company logo are fine as long as the logo is small and discrete. Choose a gift they will use over an opportunity to stick an ostentatious ad in front of them.

▶ Employees need not give gifts to employers, though a holiday card is nice. If your employer (or anyone else for that matter) bought you this book, show them you put it to good use and send them a thank you card!

BRING EXCELLENCE TO YOUR ORGANIZATION

To order bulk quantities of this book at a special rate or for information on our consulting services for your business, school, or organization please contact Modella Enterprises Inc. at info@modellabooks.com

ABOUT THE AUTHORS

Jolienne Moore is a certified Master Neuro-Linguistic-Programmer and Master Hypnotist, and is certified in Time Line Techniques and Breakthrough™ Leadership. She currently owns a talent agency and has a background in health and fitness, marketing, and business development. She is an author and facilitator specializing in the areas of personal and professional development.

Lynn Cris has a background in fashion and psychology and she is a certified Practitioner of the Art and Science of Neuro-Linguistic Programming. She is cofounder of Modella Enterprises Inc. and president of Modella Me, teaching and speaking on topics of personal development for girls and women. She focuses on increasing self-confidence and professionalism by sharing tools and techniques to help you live your life at its best!

Modella
Personal Development Program

Now Available!

Modella Me

Operate a fun and dynamic business in your community!
Specifically designed for girls aged 11-16

At Modella Me, we give you all the tools you need to start teaching the personal development program, including the use of the Modella Me name.

Your kit comes with an instructional video, marketing tools, sales book, and an in-depth teacher's manual and master copy of the student manual. You also receive online support anytime. Everything you need to get started!

Program highlights include:

Fitness/Nutrition

Manicures/Pedicures

Interview Techniques

Dining and Social Etiquette

Body language/Personality

Makeup/Hair

Reach an untapped market including summer camps, youth groups, public school system, private schools, home schooled students, families, church groups, non-profit groups and much more.

- Help prepare the girls in your region for success in whatever life path they may choose.
- Build confidence in your students so they can make important decisions and have respect for themselves and others.

Most importantly, this is a fun and interactive class that allows the students to have a great time while learning important life skills.

For more information please
visit www.ModellaMe.com or email info@modellame.com

Modella Me is a division of Modella Enterprises Inc.

BIBLIOGRAPHY

Baldrige, Letitia. New Manners for New Times. New York: Scribner, 2003

Baron, Dov. PhD, Mind Mastery. © 2007 Baron Mastery Institute

Byrne, Rhonda. The Power. Atria Books, 2010

Emoto, Masaru. The Miracle of Water. Beyond Words Publishing Inc. and Simon & Schuster 2007.

Fotinos, Joel and Gold, August. The Think and Grow Rich Workbook. Canada: Penguin Group, 2009

Holliwell, Raymond. Working With The Law.Life Success Productions, LLC 2004

www.mannersinternational.com. Manners International. 18 Nov. 2009

Modella Enterprises Dining Etiquette. Langley, BC, © 2009

Modella Enterprises. Social Etiquettes. Langley, BC, © 2009

Modella Enterprises. Wardrobe. Langley, BC, © 2009

Post, Peggy. Etiquette. 17th Edition. New York: HarperCollins, 2004

Post, Peggy & Peter. The Etiquette Advantage in Business.
New York: HarperCollins, 1999

Sharma, Robin. The Leader Who Had No Title. Free Press, 2010

Spade, Kate. Manners. Italy: Simon & Schuster, 2004

Spade, Kate. Style. Italy : Simon & Schuster, 2004

The Robinson Group. BottomLine Leadership and NLP Practioner Certification, White Rock BC. 2009

The Robinson Group. NLP Master Practitioner Certification and Breakthrough Leadership, White Rock BC. 2010

Ward, Susan. "Business etiquette quiz." 1 March 2005   <sbinfocanada. about.com/library/bizetiquettequiz/bletiquettequiz1.htm> 14 Dec. 2009

Woodall, Constantine. Trinny & Susannah What your clothes say about you. London: Weidenfeld & Nicolson, 2005.

LaVergne, TN USA
25 January 2011
213829LV00001B